T0039887

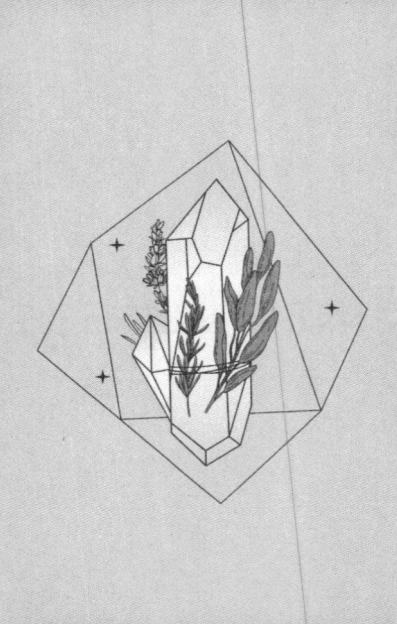

MINDFULNESS

Meditations
& Inspirations

MANDALA

San Rafael · Los Angeles · London

Be HAPPY
in the
moment.
That's
ENOUGH.

—MOTHER TERESA

Let go
of your mind,
and then be
MINDFUL.
Close your eyes
and LISTEN!

—RUMI

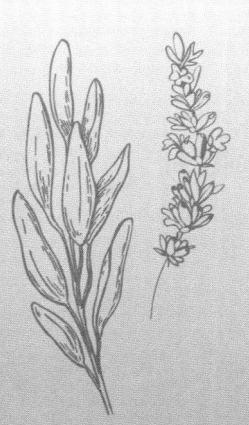

The soul aids
the body and, at
certain moments,
raises it. It is
the only bird
which bears up
its own cage.

—VICTOR HUGO

I knew life
Began where
I stood in
the DARK,
Looking out
into the
LIGHT.

—YUSEF KOMUNYAKAA

PARADISE ON EARTH IS WHERE I AM.

—Voltaire

A MIND SET IN ITS WAYS IS WASTED.

—Eric Schmidt

The mind is never right but when it is AT PEACE within itself.

—SENECA

PEOPLE DON'T GET UPSET. THEY CONTRIBUTE TO THEIR UPSETNESS.

—Albert Ellis

HAPPINESS
is where we find it, but very rarely where we seek it.

—J. Petit-Senn

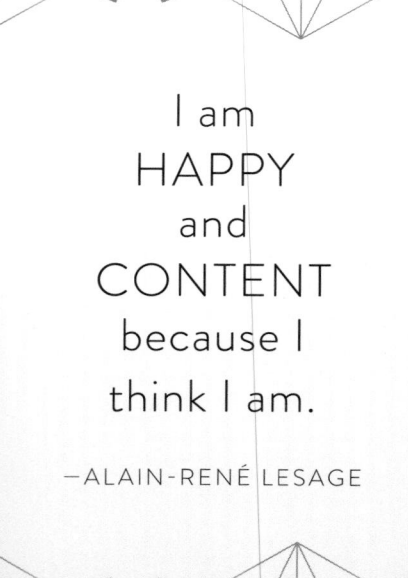

I am
HAPPY
and
CONTENT
because I
think I am.

—ALAIN-RENÉ LESAGE

Focus more on your **DESIRE** than on your **DOUBT**, and the dream will take care of itself.

—MARK TWAIN

Your MIND will answer most questions if you learn to RELAX and wait for the answer.

—WILLIAM S. BURROUGHS

AS SOON AS YOU TRUST YOURSELF,

YOU WILL KNOW HOW TO LIVE.

—Johann Wolfgang von Goethe

Anyone who reads a book with a sense of obligation does not understand the ART of reading.

—LIN YUTANG

A SIMPLE
life is

its own
REWARD.

—GEORGE SANTAYANA

The
UNEXAMINED
life is
NOT WORTH
living.

—SOCRATES

Do not
wait until the
conditions are
perfect to begin.
Beginning makes
the conditions
PERFECT.

—ALAN COHEN

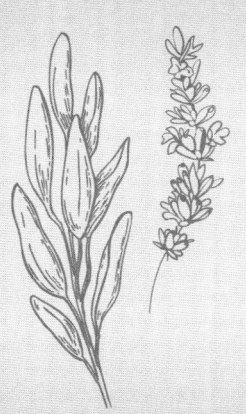

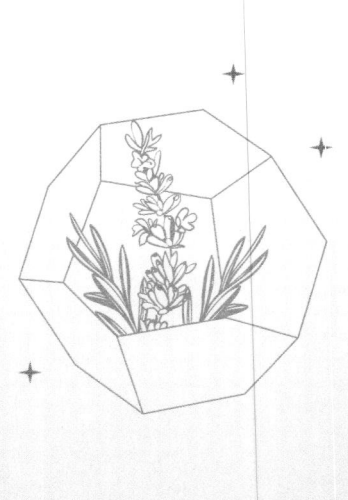

We can
never obtain
peace in
the outer world
until we make
peace with
ourselves.

—DALAI LAMA XIV

To have
the feeling,
to-day or
any day I am
SUFFICIENT
as I am!

—Walt Whitman

Mindfulness is not a mechanical process. It is developing a

very gentle, kind, and creative awareness to the present moment.

—AMIT RAY

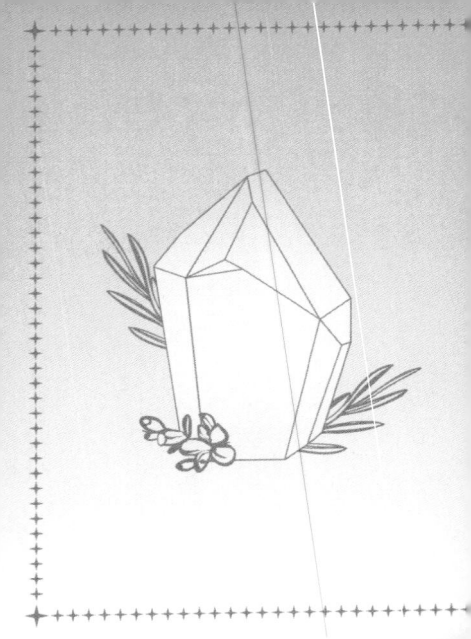

IT DOES
NOT MATTER
HOW SLOWLY
YOU GO,
AS LONG
AS YOU DO
NOT STOP.

—Confucius

The stiller you are, the calmer life is.

—RASHEED OGUNLARU

Whatever diverts
the mind from
itself may help.

—BERNARD MALAMUD

Sometimes when **FORTUNE** scowls most spitefully, she is preparing her most dazzling gifts.

—WINSTON CHURCHILL

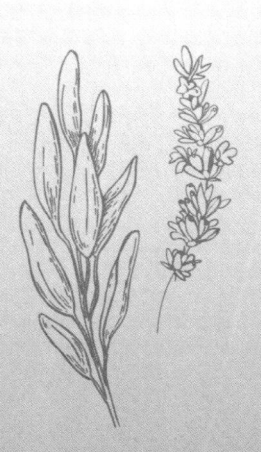

Look past your
thoughts so you
may drink the
pure nectar of
THIS MOMENT.

—RUMI

Nothing
can bring you
peace but
YOURSELF.

—RALPH WALDO
EMERSON

Life isn't about waiting for the storm to pass but learning to DANCE IN THE RAIN.

—VIVIAN GREENE

The ability to
OBSERVE
without
EVALUATING
is the highest
form of
INTELLIGENCE.

—JIDDU KRISHNAMURTI

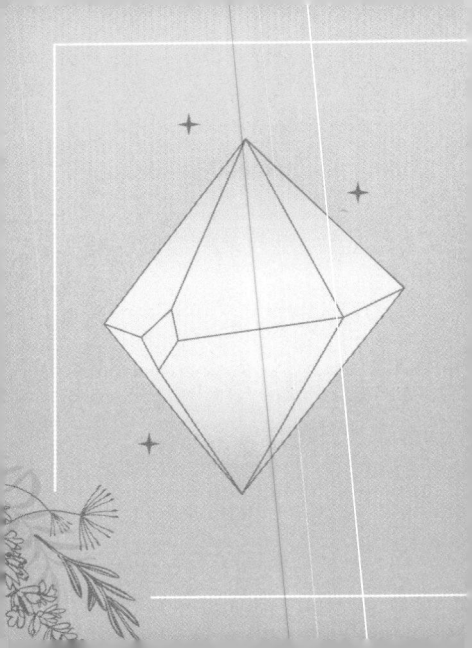

Much of spiritual life is self-acceptance, maybe all of it.

—JACK KORNFIELD

FEELINGS COME AND GO LIKE CLOUDS IN A WINDY SKY.

CONSCIOUS BREATHING IS MY ANCHOR.

—Thích Nhất Hạnh

Change your
THOUGHTS,
and you
change your
WORLD.

—NORMAN VINCENT PEALE

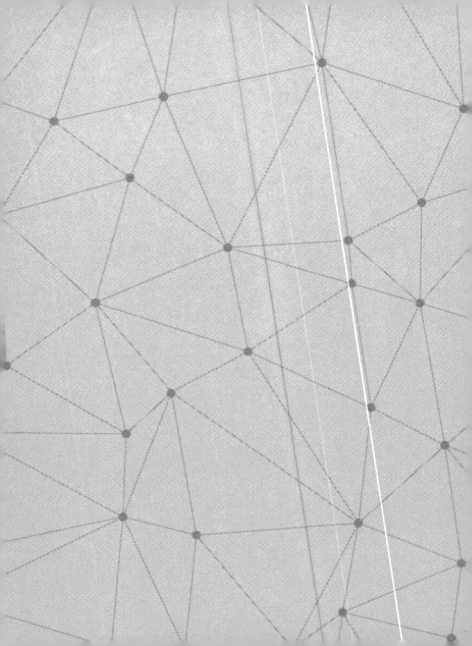

We can complain because rose bushes have thorns or rejoice because thorn bushes have roses.

—ABRAHAM LINCOLN

Distraction wastes our energy; concentration restores it.

—SHARON SALZBERG

TO THINE OWN SELF BE TRUE.

—William Shakespeare

The true secret
of happiness
lies in taking a
genuine interest
in all the details
of daily life.

—WILLIAM MORRIS

Mindfulness means being AWAKE. It means really knowing what you are doing.

—JON KABAT-ZINN

WE ARE WHAT WE REPEATEDLY DO.

EXCELLENCE, THEN, IS NOT AN ACT, BUT A HABIT.

—Will Durant

When you
press the
pause button
on a machine,
it stops.

But when you press the pause button on human beings, they start.

—DOV SEIDMAN

When we stop
RESISTING
and fighting
our thoughts
and concerns,
the battle stops.

—TAMARA LEVITT

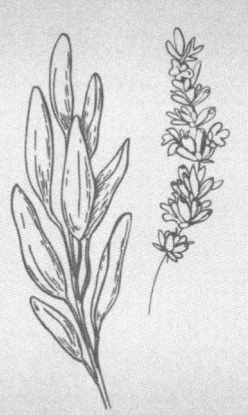

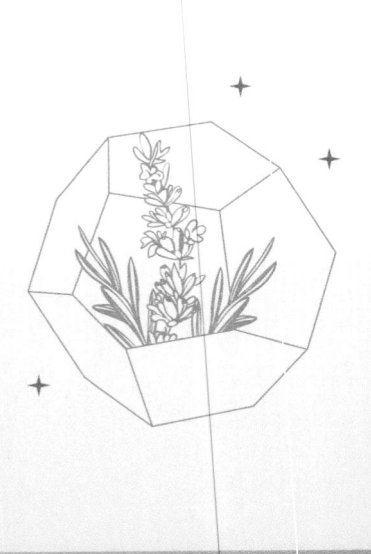

Mindfulness isn't difficult. We just need to remember to do it.

—SHARON SALZBERG

Mistakes are
the portals of
DISCOVERY.

—JAMES JOYCE

If you have
your full
attention in
the moment,
you will see
only LOVE.

—DEEPAK CHOPRA

The feeling that any task is a nuisance will soon disappear if it is done in mindfulness.

—THÍCH NHẤT HẠNH

Life has got
TO BE LIVED—
that's all
there is to it.

—ELEANOR ROOSEVELT

IF YOU THINK
YOU ARE
TOO SMALL
TO MAKE A
DIFFERENCE,

TRY SLEEPING WITH A MOSQUITO.

—DALAI LAMA XIV

You yourself,
as much as
anybody else
in the entire
universe,
deserve your
LOVE
and affection.

—SHARON SALZBERG

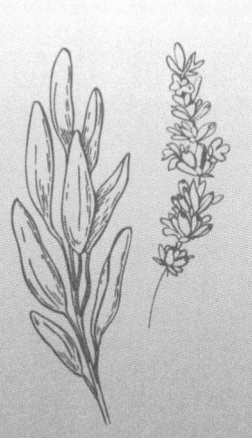

The only person
you are destined
to become is
the person you
DECIDE to be.

—RALPH WALDO
EMERSON

There are
always flowers
for those
who want to
see them.

—Henri Matisse

Our life
is shaped by
our mind, for
we BECOME
what we think.

—Buddha

If you want
to conquer
the anxiety of
life, live in the
moment, live
in the breath.

— AMIT RAY

Nowhere can a man find a quieter or more untroubled retreat than in his own SOUL.

—Marcus Aurelius

Life is not a
problem to be
solved but a
reality to be
EXPERIENCED.

—SØREN KIERKEGAARD

IT IS
NOT I WHO
CREATE
MYSELF,
RATHER I
HAPPEN TO
MYSELF.

—Carl Jung

TIME IS THE GREATEST INNOVATOR.

—Francis Bacon

Flow with whatever may happen, and let your mind be free. Stay centered by accepting whatever you are doing. This is the ultimate.

— CHUANG TZU

FINITE TO FAIL, BUT INFINITE TO VENTURE.

—EMILY DICKINSON

One moment
may with
BLISS repay
Unnumbered
hours of pain.

—THOMAS CAMPBELL

ONE TODAY IS WORTH TWO TOMORROWS.

—Benjamin Franklin

BELIEVE YOU CAN, AND YOU'RE HALFWAY THERE.

—Theodore Roosevelt

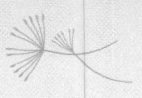

We will develop
and cultivate the
LIBERATION
of mind by
loving kindness,
make it our
vehicle,

make it our basis, stabilize it, exercise ourselves in it, and fully PERFECT IT.

—BUDDHA

What lies behind us and what lies before us are but tiny matters compared to what lies WITHIN US.

—HENRY STANLEY HASKINS

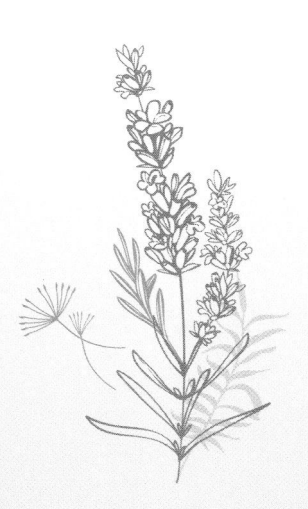

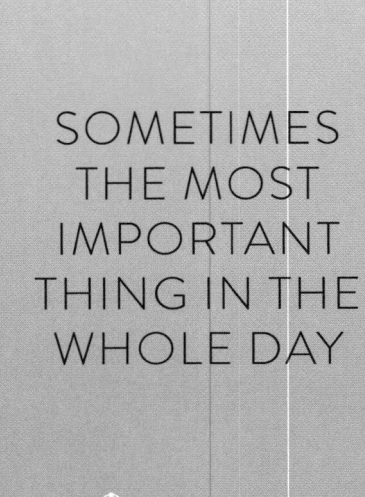

SOMETIMES
THE MOST
IMPORTANT
THING IN THE
WHOLE DAY

IS THE REST
WE TAKE
BETWEEN
TWO BREATHS.

—ETTY HILLESUM

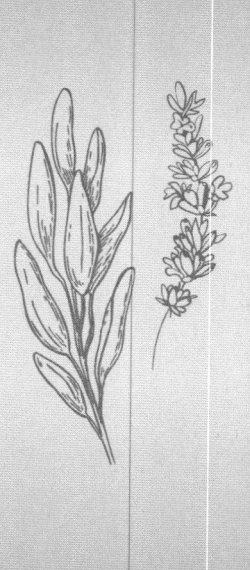

NOTHING
will work unless
YOU DO.

—Maya Angelou

As the
water beads on
a lotus leaf,
as water on
a red lily,
does not adhere,

so the sage
does not adhere
to the seen,
the heard, or
the sensed.

—BUDDHA

The very
center of your
HEART
is where life
BEGINS,
the most
beautiful place
on earth.

—RUMI

Understanding
is the
heartwood of
well-spoken
words.

—BUDDHA

The truest,
most beautiful
life never
promises to be
an easy one.

We need to
let go of the
lie that it's
supposed to be.

—GLENNON DOYLE

HOW YOU CLIMB A MOUNTAIN IS MORE

IMPORTANT
THAN
REACHING
THE TOP.

—Yvon Chouinard

The only peace, the only security, is in FULFILLMENT.

—HENRY MILLER

Sometimes, simply by sitting, the soul collects WISDOM.

—ZEN PROVERB

PARADISE

is not a place;
it's a state of
consciousness.

—SRI CHINMOY

The teacher who is indeed wise does not bid you to enter the house of his wisdom

but rather
leads you to
the threshold
of your mind.

—KAHLIL GIBRAN

Life is like riding a bicycle. To keep your BALANCE, you must keep MOVING.

—ALBERT EINSTEIN

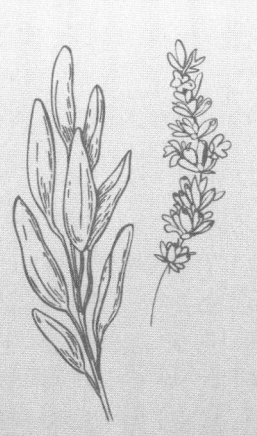

CHERISH
that which is
within you, and
SHUT OFF
that which is
without.

—Chuang Tzu

Altogether,
the idea of
MEDITATION
is not to
create states

of ecstasy or absorption, but to experience BEING.

—CHÖGYAM TRUNGPA

SOMETIMES REJECTION IN LIFE IS REALLY REDIRECTION.

—Tavis Smiley

The subconscious doesn't distinguish sarcasm and jokes. It just accepts what it hears. That's the power of words.

—INDIA ARIE

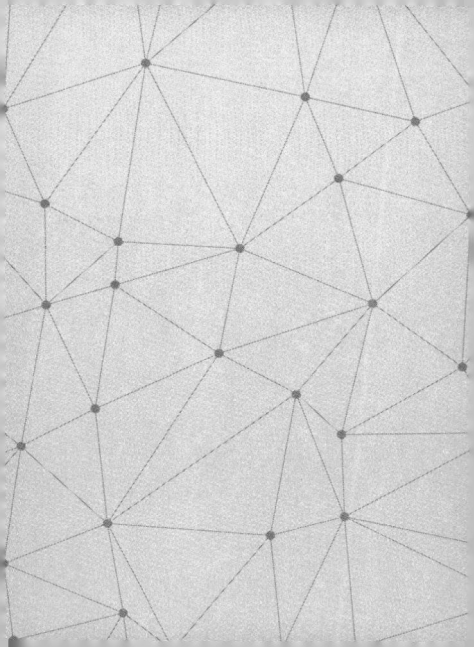

In the midst of
CHAOS,
there is also
OPPORTUNITY.

—SUN TZU

The most POWERFUL relationship you will ever have is the relationship with yourself.

—STEVE MARABOLI

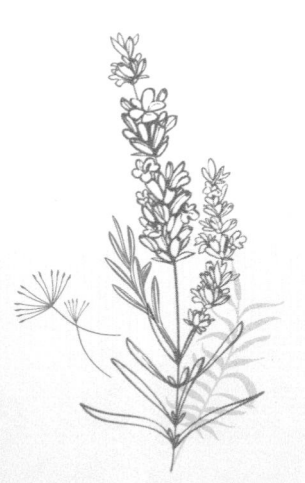

First, say to yourself what you would be, and then do what you have to do.

—Epictetus

Forget the past,
and live the
present hour.

—SARAH KNOWLES
BOLTON

TO ME, EVERY
HOUR OF
THE LIGHT
AND DARK IS
A MIRACLE,

EVERY INCH OF SPACE IS A MIRACLE.

—Walt Whitman

Don't believe everything you think. Thoughts are just that— thoughts.

—ALLAN LOKOS

How you look
at it is pretty
much how
you'll see it.

—RASHEED OGUNLARU

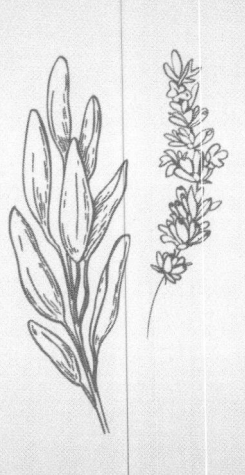

The little
THINGS?
The little
MOMENTS?
They aren't little.

—JON KABAT-ZINN

Happiness is a
butterfly which,
when pursued,
is just beyond
your grasp but,

if you will sit down
quietly, may
alight upon you.

—NATHANIEL
HAWTHORNE

Life is a dance.
Mindfulness is
WATCHING
THE DANCE.

—AMIT RAY

Wherever you are, BE THERE TOTALLY.

—ECKHART TOLLE

TRUTH
is simply
whatever you
can bring
yourself to
BELIEVE.

—ALICE CHILDRESS

Life is really simple, but we insist on making it complicated.

—CONFUCIUS

NOTHING EVER GOES AWAY UNTIL IT HAS TAUGHT US WHAT WE NEED TO KNOW.

—Pema Chödrön

It is only by
EXPRESSING
all that is
INSIDE that
purer and purer
streams come.

—BRENDA UELAND

Any fool can KNOW. The point is to UNDERSTAND.

—ALBERT EINSTEIN

He who
knows others
is clever, but
he who knows
himself is
enlightened.

—LAO TZU

LIVE ALL
YOU CAN;
IT'S A MISTAKE
NOT TO. IT
DOESN'T
SO MUCH
MATTER

WHAT YOU
DO IN
PARTICULAR,
SO LONG AS
YOU HAVE
YOUR LIFE.

—Henry James

LIFE wastes
itself while
we are
PREPARING
to live.

—Ralph Waldo Emerson

I do not want
the peace
which passeth
understanding;

I want the
understanding
which bringeth
PEACE.

—HELEN KELLER

THESE ARE
THE DAYS
THAT MUST
HAPPEN
TO YOU.

—WALT WHITMAN

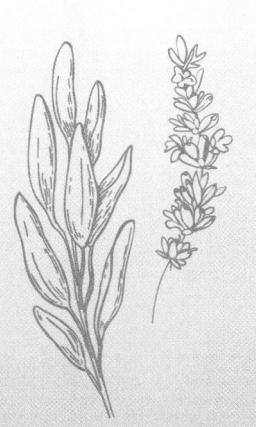

It is not what
we do once in
a while that
shapes our lives
but what we do
CONSISTENTLY.

—TONY ROBBINS

CHANGE the
way you look
at things, and
the things you
look at change.

—WAYNE DYER

THE WIND IS BLOWING. ADORE THE WIND!

—PYTHAGORAS

In truth,
to attain to
interior peace,
one must
be willing to
pass through
the contrary
to peace.

—SWAMI BRAHMANANDA

YOU CAN'T
STOP THE
WAVES,
BUT YOU
CAN LEARN
TO SURF.

—Jon Kabat-Zinn

One does
not become
ENLIGHTENED
by imagining
figures of light,
but by making
darkness
CONSCIOUS.

—CARL JUNG

Life can only
be understood
backwards, but
it must be lived
FORWARDS.

—SØREN KIERKEGAARD

WHEN I
LET GO OF
WHAT I AM,
I BECOME
WHAT I
MIGHT BE.

—Lao Tzu

The first rule
is to keep an
untroubled spirit.
The second is
to look things
in the face and
know them for
what they are.

—MARCUS AURELIUS

No great WORK has ever been produced except after a long interval of still and musing MEDITATION.

—WALTER BAGEHOT

To live is so
startling it leaves
little time for
anything else.

—EMILY DICKINSON

There can be no peace without, but through peace within.

—WILLIAM ELLERY CHANNING

BE HAPPY
FOR THIS
MOMENT.
THIS
MOMENT IS
YOUR LIFE.

—Omar Khayyam

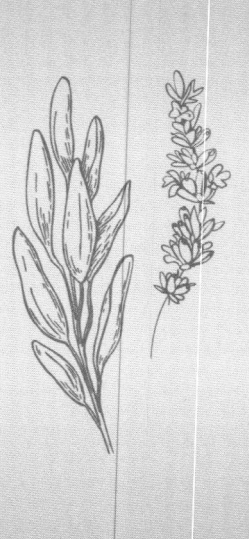

PATIENCE is not the ability to wait but how you act while you're waiting.

—JOYCE MEYER

The SECRET
of contentment
is knowing how
to enjoy what
you have and

to be able to

lose all desires

for things

BEYOND

YOUR REACH.

—LIN YUTANG

YOU ARE THE SKY. EVERYTHING ELSE IS JUST THE WEATHER.

—Pema Chödrön

WE OWN
NO PAST,
NO FUTURE,
WE ONLY
POSSESS
NOW.

—Mary Baker Eddy

Only when your consciousness is totally focused on the MOMENT you are in

can you receive
whatever gift,
lesson, or delight
that moment
has to offer.

—BARBARA DE ANGELIS

I AM AN EXPRESSION OF THE DIVINE.

—Alice Walker

Being satisfied
and grateful
with what we
already have is a
magical golden

key to being
alive in a full,
unrestricted, and
inspired way.

—PEMA CHÖDRÖN

RESOLUTELY TRAIN YOURSELF TO ATTAIN PEACE.

—Buddha

WE FORGET
THE CHAINS
WE WEAR
IN LIFE.

—CHARLES DICKENS

When you bow,
you should
JUST BOW;
when you sit,
you should JUST
SIT; when you
eat, you should
JUST EAT.

—SHUNRYU SUZUKI

I DWELL IN POSSIBILITY.

—Emily Dickinson

You must
be completely
awake in the
PRESENT to
enjoy the tea.

—THÍCH NHẤT HẠNH

The ultimate GIFT of conscious life is a sense of the MYSTERY that encompasses it.

—LEWIS MUMFORD

THINKING
ABOUT
INTERIOR
PEACE
DESTROYS
INTERIOR
PEACE.

THE PATIENT WHO CONSTANTLY FEELS HIS PULSE IS NOT GETTING ANY BETTER.

—Hubert van Zeller

You cannot control the RESULTS, only your ACTIONS.

—Allan Lokos

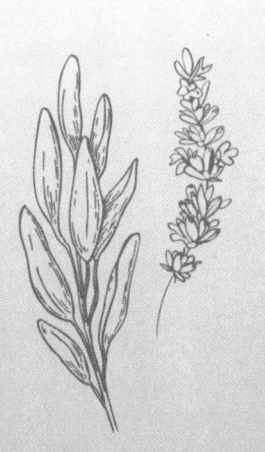

A man who dares to waste one hour of life has not discovered the value of life.

—CHARLES DARWIN

If there is to
be any PEACE,
it will come
through being,
not having.

—HENRY MILLER

LIVING
WELL AND
BEAUTIFULLY
AND JUSTLY
ARE ALL ONE
THING.

—Socrates

Every time we
become aware
of a thought,
as opposed to
being lost in
a thought,

we experience
that OPENING
of THE MIND.

—JOSEPH GOLDSTEIN

WAVES ARE THE PRACTICE OF WATER.

—Shunryu Suzuki

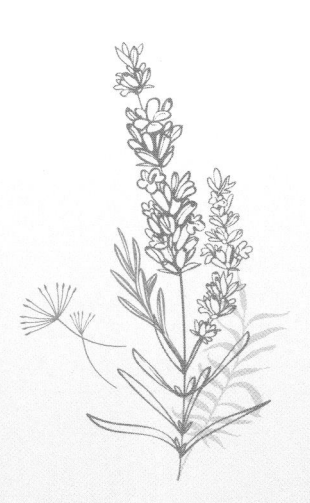

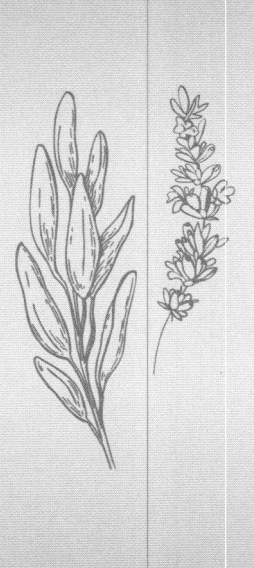

Happiness is when what you think, what you say, and what you do are in HARMONY.

—MAHATMA GANDHI

Surrender is
a journey from
the outer turmoil
to the
INNER PEACE.

—SRI CHINMOY

Happiness is your nature. It is not wrong to desire it.

What is wrong
is seeking it
outside when
it is inside.

—RAMANA MAHARSHI

There is something wonderfully bold and liberating about saying YES to our entire imperfect and messy life.

—TARA BRACH

SMILE,
BREATHE,
AND GO
SLOWLY.

—Thích Nhất Hạnh

In this moment, there is plenty of time. In this moment, you are precisely as you should be.

To know what you know and what you do not know, that is true knowledge.

—CONFUCIUS

In this moment, there is INFINITE POSSIBILITY.

—VICTORIA MORAN

WITH THE NEW DAY COMES NEW STRENGTH AND NEW THOUGHTS.

—Eleanor Roosevelt

There's only one corner of the universe you can be certain of improving,

and that's your
OWN SELF.

—ALDOUS HUXLEY

If you aren't in the moment, you are either looking FORWARD to uncertainty or BACK to pain and regret.

—JIM CARREY

IN ANY
MOMENT,
we can find
grounding in
the breath.

—TAMARA LEVITT

He who knows all the ANSWERS has not been asked all the QUESTIONS.

—CONFUCIUS

A journey
of a thousand
miles begins
with a single
STEP.

—LAO TZU

IT IS A PEACEFUL THING TO BE THE ONE SUCCEEDING.

—Gertrude Stein

Learn silence. With the quiet serenity of a meditative mind, listen, absorb, transcribe, and transform.

—PYTHAGORAS

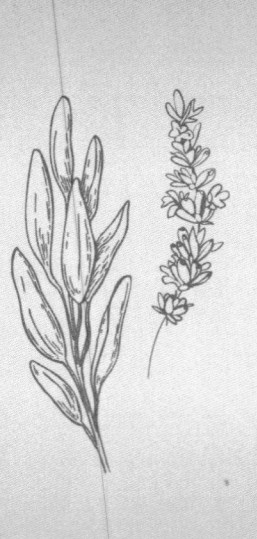

Put your
HEART, MIND,
and SOUL
into even your
smallest acts.
This is the secret
of success.

—SWAMI SIVANANDA

You leave old habits behind by starting out with the thought,

"*I release the
need for this
in my life.*"

—WAYNE DYER

YOUR
HEART IS
THE SIZE OF
AN OCEAN.

GO FIND
YOURSELF IN
ITS HIDDEN
DEPTHS.

—Rumi

If you can't
change your
FATE,
change your
ATTITUDE.

—AMY TAN

MANDALA

Mandala Publishing
P.O. Box 3088
San Rafael, CA 94912
www.mandalaearth.com

CEO: Raoul Goff
Editorial Director: Katie Killebrew
VP Creative: Chrissy Kwasnik
VP Manufacturing: Alix Nicholaeff
Associate Art Director: Ashley Quackenbush
Designer: Lola Villanueva
Project Editor: Claire Yee
Production Manager: Andy Harper

ISBN: 978-1-64722-578-0
Manufactured in China by Insight Editions
10 9 8 7 6 5 4 3 2 1
2022 2023 2024